7 MBA Application Tips:

Stop Sending Pointless Applications and Instantly Get into Your School of Choice

Garland P. Brackins

7 MBA Application Tips: 1

Introduction 3

Chapter 1: Fundamentals of an Application 6

Chapter 2: Choosing an MBA Program 11

   Types of Schools to Apply To 11

   Looking at Individual MBA Programs 14

Chapter 3: Standing Out in the Crowd 19

   What Could Be Your "Wow" Factor? 23

Chapter 4: Essay Preparation 25

   How Should I Get Started? 25

Chapter 5: Interview Preparation 32

   Some Common Questions to Prepare For 37

Chapter 6: Strategies for Better Essay Writing 44

Chapter 7: Know Your Audience 48

Conclusion 51

Introduction

Congratulations on downloading *7 MBA Application Tips*! If you are reading this book, you more than likely have a goal to get into a great business school of your choice. The application process can be daunting and time-consuming. With applications to fill out, resumes to write, and essays to perfect, it can become easy to get stressed out about the process. With this book, we will guide you and give you the best tips for you to stand out in the crowd.

Your application is all about letting your professional, academic, and personal strengths shine. You have accomplished a lot to get to this point. Your undergraduate transcript and test scores will speak for themselves. They are obviously critical factors for an admission committee. But let's be honest—most applicants probably have very similar scores and GPAs. It can be tough to think of a unique factor that can help you stand out. That's where this book helps you recognize your strengths and elaborate on your personal experiences.

We'll even help you with deciding which tier schools to apply to—your dream schools, safety schools, or target schools. You want to aim high but at the same time, remain realistic when it comes to your test scores and school GPA. Maybe you are overwhelmed with how many choices there are of business programs out there. We have a comprehensive list that can help you narrow down your choices based on what attributes you are looking for. What kind of faculty does the school have? What are its facilities like? Have you talked to a recent alumna/alumnus about the program? Have you taken a look at the school's job placement numbers of recent graduates? Where is it located, and have you done your research on the area? All these factors can help you make your decision about a program.

With a strong writing style and following some tips to polish your essay, you can be sure to stand out in a crowd of applicants. When it comes to preparing your essay and practicing your interview, we have provided you tips to get organized and motivate yourself for success. One of the most important things you can do is have enough time to prepare. Even if you are a strong writer and speaker, the interview format could be something you are not familiar with. Some schools are doing team-based interviews where you work with other applicants to solve a real-world problem. Or it could be the more traditional one-on-one interview format you are expecting. With our tips on how to communicate with the interviewer and composing your thoughts articulately, you can feel confident that you've given a great impression and conveyed your desires well to attend their school. We have nearly a dozen sample interview questions for you to plan your answers concisely to avoid rambling.

Our writing tips will help you when it comes to your essay. No two essays will be the same because each is going to convey details about your unique history and personality. Be sure you have examples if asked to share about your leadership or teamwork skills. Don't ramble or repeat the same story, and avoid using "fancy" dictionary words or technical jargon that would confuse the reader and muddle your essay. You want to be clear when it comes to your thoughts and conveying your motivation for getting into school. With our tips, you will feel confident about your essay and your application and feel like you can get into your dream school.

There are plenty of books on this subject on the market, but thank you for choosing this one.

Chapter 1: Fundamentals of an Application

After graduating from college and gaining valuable skills and insights through your studies and activities, it's time for the next step—business school. Before you begin the grueling process of filling out MBA applications, it's important that you understand all the aspects involved. Filing periods can be anywhere from six to nine months. Some schools can use rounds dividing the filing period to cycles in a year, others will have rolling admission where they review applications as received. Be sure you've looked into the policy of the schools you are interested in. This will give you an idea of what your deadline looks like and how many applications you will need to be working on at one time.

What are the other parts of your application process that you need to be aware of? Below we list some of them. This is merely a general list, and some schools can require more specific documents. It's your responsibility to look at the actual list and what deadlines may be applicable.

Transcript: As we are well aware, your undergraduate transcript and overall GPA will play a big part in your application. Not only will schools want to look at the reputation of your college, as well as the selection and rigor of the classes you took but they are also going to evaluate your overall performance. Some business schools may look more closely at your junior-year or senior-year grades. But this is not a rule, and you should be prepared that it's your overall GPA that will be looked at. Schools will look at your quantitative courses like economics, statistics, and calculus, which are good indicators of your strong success in grad school. This should be something that you have already discussed with your guidance counselor when it comes to your major and future plans.

Standardized test scores: The majority of the MBA programs in the country will require you to have taken the GRE or GMAT test. Check and see if a school requires one specifically or both. Even if you've taken the test more than once, schools will generally look at your most recent score. A great test score is a factor that can boost your application, but it shouldn't be the only thing you count on when it comes to your application being accepted. (We should, however, warn you that a low score will more than likely keep you from getting accepted. Be sure you speak with your guidance counselor for further advice if you fall into this category. Consider retaking the test if you did not do well on the first try.) Check your business school's profile to see what scores on average they accept and how you compare.

Resume: The typical application will have nearly five to ten years of professional experience, counting the undergraduate and high school years and any gap years that may have been taken. You want your resume to reflect your accomplishments and any special team-building experiences to highlight your strengths in leadership roles. Point out things you've been a part of like volunteer roles, community projects, or other notable activities. Follow advice from your counselor regarding a good resume format and leave out anything extraneous that can seem like you are filling it with "fluff."

Letters of Recommendation: Admission officers require recommendation letters to get a stronger sense of who you are as an applicant and how you are portraying yourself. An academic reference should be someone who can comment on your performance from an academic setting, like a mentor or a club advisor. You don't want to try and get the famous professor to write a letter if they don't actually know you or have interacted with you well enough to get an idea of your academic goals and successes. For a professional reference, find someone who can evaluate your performance in other activities you are involved in. A more personal letter from someone you worked closely with is more impactful than having the CEO sign off on a common "cookie cutter" letter that isn't specific to you. You can give your preparers a general idea of what theme you are looking for and reminders of what projects or activities you were involved in that can highlight your strengths. Make sure you give them enough time to complete the request. You don't want to spring the letter on them with a short deadline where they don't have enough time to compose a few drafts and think out their ideas.

Essays: Just as it was an important part of your undergraduate application, your MBA application essay is also an important part of your portfolio and showcases your strengths as a writer and your overall personality. Admission committees are looking for students who shine in their essays. They want a unique, well-rounded, strong essay that has a great topic to keep them engaged and that showcases a strong writing style. They want to feel like they're choosing a positive individual with potential at the school, both in and out of the classroom. They want to feel like you are focused and dedicated to this dream that you are aiming for. Topics for the essays can be varied depending on what your school requires. They could ask you to describe yourself or a memory unique to you or why you want to pursue your dreams of getting an MBA at this particular school.

Interview: Along with the application process, schools may use personal interview to screen applicants. Some schools require an interview so they can have a more real impression of a person beyond the grades and scores, while other schools use it to decide between "maybe" applicants. Be sure to quickly schedule an appointment if one is required. You don't want spots to fill up and ruin your chances or have your admission delayed. You should look up some interview tips that'll guide you on how to properly behave and dress up and provide you with strong answers for potential questions.

As we said above, this is a general list of what most schools require, but some schools may have more specific details. Be sure you've taken the time to look at each school's individual requirements and their deadlines.

Chapter 2: Choosing an MBA Program

When you are trying to put together a list of which MBA programs you will apply to, it's possible that you have a mental hurricane of questions invading your brain—everything from which school you will get into to, costs and financial aid, from location to ranking, and reputation—including how to know if it's the perfect school for you. There are lots of factors to consider, and we're going to briefly go through some with you so you can make an informed decision.

Types of Schools to Apply To

First, when it comes to applying for schools, you are probably debating how many and what types of schools you should apply to. An application process is lengthy and requires time, effort, and money. We recommend picking a mix of schools that offer you a competitive edge and academic compatibility. Here's a great breakdown below:

- **Dream schools**: Aim high! Just like every student aiming for a dream career, you want to try and get into the best school you can. Instead of focusing on schools you only think you can get into, aim high for the best schools like Wharton, Stanford, or Harvard. Your personal fit to a school is always going to be the deciding factor, but don't limit yourself based on your biased opinion of your weaknesses. Chances are if you've been serious about your dream of applying to an MBA school, you are most likely a strong applicant who would be a great addition to any prestigious program. If you don't give yourself a chance and apply to your dream school, you'll never know! Sure, many programs are very selective and have an acceptance rate in the single digits, but you'll never know if you don't try. We're not saying that you should waste a lot of money on top-tier schools if you don't have the strong application to back it up, but don't write them off until you at least try. If your application is a little weak with regard to test scores, you can consider taking the GMAT or GRE again. If you have some academic weaknesses, have a strong essay and letters of recommendation to showcase your other strengths.

- **Target schools**: These are the schools that you want to attend and where you feel you have a chance at getting into. You want to look at each school's admission statistics to see where your application would fall. Look at your undergraduate GPA, your GRE or GMAT test scores, your credentials for work and volunteering. Don't rule out a school if a few things fall short of credentials because many other factors can apply to give your application a well-rounded view for admission counselors. You also want to be sure that these are schools you would be excited to go to. Chances are if you are picking these schools, you've done your research into factors that would excite you. If you are going to be at the school for two years, you want to feel secure in your decision.

- **Safety schools**: These are the schools you consider to have a high chance of being admitted because your application is more likely better than the school's admission statistics. Regardless of the school, you want to think of it as a place that you wouldn't mind attending. Think of it this way: if you had to suddenly leave your first choice school and attend the safety school, you would need to be happy with that choice. Safety schools don't mean they're less desirable to you or that they're bad schools—they're simply a more obvious fit to your application profile. Keep in mind, though, that viewing a school as a safety school does not guarantee your admission. You still need to apply with a strong application, and each school will judge you based on your personality, essay, test scores, and overall application. It happens sometimes that you get into a more competitive school and get denied by a less competitive one. Each school has different requirements, and you never know how an admission committee will compare applications. It's always good not to get your hopes up regarding a school, even a safety one.

Looking at Individual MBA Programs

When it comes to looking at specific schools and the programs you are interested in, there are many factors you want to consider that are going to define the school of your choice. Each school is going to be unique and will offer factors that could or could not match your school requirement list. Here are some factors you may want to consider carefully:

- **Program:** First and foremost, you want to focus on the program that you are applying for. What does the school offer in terms of your ambitions for an MBA? What areas does the school focus in? What rank is the program given? What are the specific strengths unique to this program? Is it going to provide you with all the necessary skills and confidence to enter the postgrad school professional world? What are the official statistics on graduation and employment rate? Your ideal school should have all the requirements that you need and everything you aspire to have when it comes to your future career. Don't let it fall short of your dreams.

- **Rankings**: Though it may not be the most important criteria for some people, you do want to view a school's ranking and accreditation to have an idea of where it stands in the wider world of education and business. Each school should have at least one accreditation by an international corporation—EQUIS, AMBA, or AACSB. There are going to be other factors involved when you make your decision, but a ranking gives you an idea of where the school fits in the larger community and how it is perceived. Take them with a grain of salt, but do your research with multiple sources to see where schools rank and why.

- **Size**: Depending on the size of your undergraduate school, you might have a preference for the size of MBA school you want to attend. Or maybe you are looking for a change and wanting to try a completely different environment. A school can have over a thousand students admitted into the program or a mere 20 or 30 students. The size of a school will depend on the resources it has access to. A smaller program can offer more intimacy between the students and the faculty, while a larger one can offer you access to more faculty and opportunities. It's all about doing research on the school and finding out what works for you.

- **Location**: If you are going to be working on your degree online or only part-time, this won't be as important for you as it is for a full-time student. But a school's location is going to be important for those who need to be on campus or who need to commute. Maybe there's a region in the country you prefer or a particular location in mind based on your career prospects. It could be that a specific region or a particular location will have more of the opportunities that you are aiming for, like technology and software jobs in California or finance related jobs in New York. If you are going to be making a big move, make sure you've done your research on the campus and be familiar with the location. Don't forget about the weather too!

- **Career Planning**: As today's job market becomes more competitive, this should be an important factor when considering which school to choose. Your MBA is going to be an asset, but you want to be sure your school can help you with landing a job in the professional field. Schools will have a guidance office and counselors who will assess your progress and help you when the time comes for applying for internships and jobs. You want to be sure that your school has a dedicated business career center that attracts recruiters and connects you with great opportunities for placement.

- **Faculty**: It's easy to have your choice of school be influenced by any star-power faculty members, like famous entrepreneurs or influencers. But know what the likelihood is of you interacting with these individuals or having any one-on-one time with them. You want to look more at the overall staff to get an idea of the kind of staff the university employs. This will be more helpful to have positive relationships with teachers and have a mentor who can guide you through your schooling. Talk to previous students of the school to see how they felt about the faculty and how approachable they were to their students. More than just a famous name, you want to walk away from the school feeling enriched and supported by your teachers and professors.

- **Culture**: Do some research into the individual culture the school will provide you. Whether it is campus life, activities, and clubs, or a classroom setting, you are going to be spending a lot of time on campus if you are a full-time student and engaging in classes, so you want to feel comfortable with the school's style. Whether you want a competitive environment or a more collegiate one or one with lots of mandatory activities or one with no club life, you want to be sure you are choosing a school you feel you can enjoy and excel at.

These are all factors that you should consider when choosing schools and picking your dream, safety, and target schools. You want to aim high to ensure you get into the best school you can, but be realistic with your application profile and where you stand overall. This process is subjective, and admission counselors will want to see more of your personality than the demographic facts. But your performance will matter as they decide on the incoming class. Apply to a nice mix of schools so you can have a target school and a safety for backup. Be sure that you like all the schools on your list because you don't want to waste your time and money applying to somewhere you would not want to go. Most people recommend at least seven schools—two dream schools, three target schools, and two safety schools. Have a smart selection strategy and a short list when it comes to your schools as the process is becoming more and more competitive.

Chapter 3: Standing Out in the Crowd

As you are applying for your MBA programs, it can seem daunting when you realize that there are going to be thousands of other similarly qualified applicants who are also applying. With so many applicants who have the same professional histories and transcript credentials, how are you going to stand out from the crowd? What makes you the best candidate? What would an admission committee find appealing about you on a personal level?

We know it will sound like a cliché, but every admission counselor's first piece of advice will be to be yourself. Schools want to get an idea of the kind of person they could be admitting—an idea more than just transcript grades or test scores. If you are going to be an active member of the student body for the next two years, admission counselors want an idea of your personality and your strengths and how you'll enrich their campus. Keep this in mind even as you agonize about standing out from the crowd!

Here are some more tips to guide you when it comes to your application.

Have a story. When submitting an application, you are in theory selling yourself. You want to highlight yourself and your strengths and what sets you apart from the crowd. Share about the things that inspire you and have motivated you for this dream of business school. Share what has guided you in your life to make the decisions you've made and why you've chosen this path. It can require some reflection to highlight yourself and your unique qualities, something that most humble people will have difficulty with. Try creating a "brag sheet" as inspiration about what you've accomplished and how hard you've worked. Focus on your professional successes, but don't be afraid to touch upon your personal side and the people, organizations, or services that have inspired you. Think about your life and what has shaped you. Has there been an obstacle you've had to overcome? Does your family have any interesting traditions? What are your plans for the future? Is there a community organization you've been involved in that motivates you?

Show yourself as a well-rounded individual. Yes, you are applying and rooting for your professional future, but schools want an idea about the type of person you are overall and what you will add to their community. Of course, you want to highlight your academic and professional successes, but don't forget to discuss who you are as a person. Talk about your hobbies or volunteering services. Talk about your family members and what inspires you or the people who have motivated you on your journey. Schools want a diverse student body—people from different educational and professional backgrounds, nontraditional students, students who have taken a few years off to get life experience. They want interesting people! Highlight the layers you have and how you hope to enrich your life with business school even further.

Show your leadership strengths. Admission counselors love problem solvers and having people who are strong leaders and take charge. Use your application to highlight your strengths if you've been a leader in your academic or professional career. Were you the president of a club at college? Did you take ownership and lobby against your local government about a controversial law? Did you start a charity for a good cause? Whatever it is that you've accomplished, highlight that as a cause you championed for and the initiative that you took for the idea to materialize. Connect this with your plans in business school and how you want to continue to be a strong leader in the community.

Show that you are a team player. It might seem counterintuitive when we just told you to highlight your strengths as a leader, but admission counselors also want to know that you understand the importance of a team. It's not always simply about yourself! You want to highlight that you understand your role in a larger group and community and that you are respectful and able to work with many types of people in challenging settings. Your cooperation skills should be emphasized in your application, especially when it comes to things like volunteering or assisting in local community projects. Even a personal experience can highlight your ability to communicate and work well with others, like organizing a blood drive at your church or creating a diversity club on campus. Use these skills to highlight your excitement about the school you are applying to and how you want to incorporate yourself into that community, whether it's joining new clubs, rooting for the football team, or partaking in school traditions.

What Could Be Your "Wow" Factor?

Professional

- Do you have a specific expertise that can help you with business school?
- Do you have a special role in the workplace that you feel would tie well into your application?
- Do you have any stories of leadership regarding projects you've pulled off at work?
- Do you have a military background that has shaped you into the person you are?

Extra-Curricular Services

- Are there causes special to you that you work for and that motivate you? Be sure they're included in your resume and that you write about them.
- What impact have you left on the world, and how do you want to use your MBA plans to make more of a difference?

Personal

- Is there something unique about your upbringing or childhood that you feel shaped you? Pick something that can be an interesting story.

- What have you tried and failed, and how did that motivate you for success?
- Who have been the people who motivated you, and how are you inspired by them?
- What character traits do you feel set you apart from the industry?

Chapter 4: Essay Preparation

When it comes to your MBA application essay, a lot of the same tips that make your overall application stand out apply (see the previous chapter). The essay is a way in which committees gain personal insight into the applicants; they want to see the person beyond the test scores and transcripts. You want to focus on writing about the issues that are personal to you and can highlight your successes in the professional or academic environment or ones that showcase your personal hobbies or extracurricular activities that shape you as a person. Schools want well-rounded individuals who can excel both professionally and personally at their school.

Here are some tips to get you started as you sit to tackle your application essay.

How Should I Get Started?

- **Brainstorm**: Answer the question. First and foremost, you want to be sure you are direct in answering the application essay question. Whether it's asking you to reflect on your flaws or about the hurdles you've encountered or for a time you showed leadership strength or who has motivated you on your academic path, have a direct answer, and then begin to build your essay around that. If you use a lot of flowery language but don't directly answer the question, chances are admission counselors would not be impressed.

- **Reflect**: Think about your own life and academic career and how you can answer the question. What are the goals that you've accomplished that fit this question? What experiences make you unique that you can tell the committee about? What is the most important factor of your motivation and drive that you want the committee to know about? Think back on your life and your academic career to share what has been special and monumental in shaping you.

- **Design**: Start to frame your essay in terms of the question and your experiences that correspond with it. Start with a bullet point version and details of the events or people you want to write about. Work your way out as you expand. Don't be limited by the word count for your first draft—you want to get your ideas out and then go back and edit for length and structure.

Here are some tips to help you with the essay process.

Write as much as you can first without worrying about the word count. Yes, a school is going to have a word limit so your essay is kept concise. But as you are starting to brainstorm, don't limit yourself when trying to convey your message. Write as much as you need and then be prepared to go back and edit for word count. The more passionate and honest you are about the subject matter, the more you will be able to write and show enthusiasm about yourself. You can always edit for length, instead of trying to fill an essay with "fluff."

Give specifics when asked. If a question is asking for examples of your leadership or teamwork experiences, then be sure to give specific instances and how you were involved. Name the company involved, the group or charity that you worked with, what your leadership role was, and what you managed to accomplish when you took charge or initiated a change. When it comes to shining a light on your strengths, you want to be as specific as you can so admission committees can have an idea of your successes.

Don't be afraid to show your personal side. Admission counselors have all the statistics on your transcript and test scores to see how you've succeeded academically, but they also want to get to know the people who will be joining their student body. If an essay question dives into the personal side of your life, take some time to reflect about how you've matured and what path your life has taken to get you to where you are today. What would you be comfortable writing about? What events have shaped you and motivated you when it comes to applying to this school?

Highlight your unique diversity. Colleges want to have a diverse incoming class with students from different backgrounds and atmospheres. There are going to be many differences between students who have taken the traditional path of high school and undergraduate school versus students who took time off for a gap year and students who were in the military or studied abroad. If you feel there is something unique in your background like your cultural identity or personal experiences, then talk about those factors and how they make you stand out.

Take time to showcase your interests and hobbies. This has to do with the aspect of taking the time to show your personal side. If you have specific hobbies or you are involved in a club or an organization or you volunteer for or work with a charity, then mention these in your essay and highlight the time and enthusiasm you put into these causes. This will give admission counselors a strong sense of your communication skills, community involvement, problem-solving and teamwork skills, and ethics. These are the traits that colleges want to see in a well-rounded individual.

Avoid technical language, clichés, and flowery language. Using technical or business jargon might seem like an appropriate idea since you are of course applying to a business school, but you don't want your essay to come off as another extension of who you are professionally or academically. You want to appear more approachable and personable.

Use your best writing skills. Just like your undergraduate application essay, you also want your MBA application essay to be an example of strong writing. If writing isn't a natural skill for you, don't be afraid to get advice from your guidance counselors or school writing center or from family and friends who can help you. There's no shame in writing a few drafts first so you can assess which reads the strongest. Include some humor and empathy in the paper and be sure you are varying your sentence structures so it's a more engaging read for the admission committee. Read it out loud before you submit it so you have an idea of how the words flow and if anything sounds off.

Use different essays for each school. We know the application period is a lengthy, stressful process, but we urge you not to take an essay, search, and copy and paste the name of another college, and submit it to that school. You want your essays to be specific to the school you are applying for. If you feel you can do a quick "copy and paste" and use that essay for multiple schools, then you probably haven't personalized it enough. You want to have a unique essay for each school so they feel as if you are truly devoting the time and energy for their application.

Start early so you have plenty of time to revise. Writing can be a tough process for some people, especially because of the pressure that comes with writing a stellar application essay. You want to be sure you have time to revise your draft and go over it for sentence structure, spelling, word count, and content. You may want to have your guidance counselor or school's writing center read it and give you feedback or ask a family member or friend for their opinion. Improving the first draft takes time, so you want to be sure you aren't scrambling and simply sending in something uncompleted before the deadline. Especially when it comes to more personal topics and "selling yourself," you want to have time to reflect on your journey and your accomplishments.

Respect the word count. Even if you have a great essay that's just a little over the word count guideline, we'd urge you to stay within the boundaries. Some schools may allow a slight deviation, 5–10% more words, but most advisors would tell you to stay within the limit. Avoid repetition in your essay and try to be concise as much as possible while still channeling your positivity and enthusiasm. Editing your essay multiple times can help you remove any repeated words or phrases. And let's be honest, we all have blind spots when it comes to our own work, so it's a great idea to have a few people review your essay to provide you feedback. After you've been working on multiple essays for weeks at a time, it can be refreshing to have another person to read your work.

Chapter 5: Interview Preparation

If you've received an interview invite by a school, that's a great sign that they want to learn more about you and get a first impression! Competition can be fierce, but the interview is your place to shine and give a great impression of the type of personality you want to bring to the school.

Even if you are confident about your public speaking and interview skills, you still want to prepare for the interview. Schools will be looking at how you articulate your answers, the way you compose your thoughts when given unexpected questions, how you explain your leadership and teamwork skills, and how you explain your career ambitions. The interview is almost like a test of authenticity—does the person you are match with what you've depicted in your application and essay? Are you honest and truthful about your goals and what your path has been?

Here are some interview tips to help you prepare.

Know what kind of interview format you'll undergo. With a growing competitive environment, schools have been changing their interview formats to keep applicants on their toes. There are many new techniques and formats in order for admission counselors to get a better idea of the people they are interviewing. At Stanford Business School, you might have an hour-long, blind interview with some alumni/alumnae. The interviewers will only browse your resume and make their impression of you solely from how you answer questions and compose yourself. Wharton Business School has been known to have team-based interviews that bring together candidates and make them solve a real-world business scenario. This allows interviewers to observe how you operate in a team setting and how well you work with others. It can be nerve-wracking to know you are being watched the entire time. Some schools will have the more traditional one-on-one interview slot where you speak more intimately with a counselor and sell yourself and your application. Whatever the format is, it's important that you are aware of what format you are preparing for. Be sure to ask people who have attended the school and the admission department for as much information as they can give you. You only have one chance to make a great first impression, so you want to know what the situation will be like when you step into that room.

Take the time to practice. Even if you have confidence in your ability to wow the other person in the room, you still want to take some time to prepare your answers. You will have to speak without hesitation and without words that ruin your flow such as "um" or "like" or "uh." You want to have a good elaborate answer for common questions like "tell me about yourself" or "tell me about the academic experiences on your resume." You want to have a response prepared so you aren't scrambling on the spot. You want to seem calm and relaxed as you answer the questions. Have your answers in bullet points so it gives you a guide and conduct a mock interview with family or friends for feedback. Another great tip is to record the mock interview so you can review it and see what sort of impression you've made. This can give an idea of your weaknesses and how you can better fill any gaps or awkward pauses in your answer.

Don't forget your appearance. Just like in any professional interview, you want to be sure you've taken the time to plan your outfit and look presentable in appropriate business attire. For men that will mean a suit with a tie, and for women a skirt and blouse combination or a dress. Avoid flashy colors or patterns. Following up the interview with a personalized thank you note adds a great touch as well.

Listen and don't interrupt. Regardless of the lively tone of conversation or how well you seem to be getting on with the interviewer, you still want to remain in a humble position and not interrupt or speak out of turn. You want to focus on the person who is talking and wait until they complete their question before you begin answering. Listen to what is really being asked and don't hesitate to ask if they can repeat it if you were unsure. This can stop you from giving a confused or indirect answer.

Keep a pleasant, professional tone. Humility always works better as a persona than arrogance. Yes, you are going to have to sell yourself and your accomplishments, but you don't want to come off as a haughty person. Avoid giving cute or cliché responses and stay professional and friendly. Don't share doubts about yourself, your abilities, or the program you are applying for. You want to remain positive about yourself and your resume and not allow insecurities to filter through.

Expect the unexpected. Schools are going to want to test you and see how you react to confrontation or to being challenged with respect to your answers. If questions keep coming back to something in particular, you want to stay calm and continue to give confident responses. You need to be prepared to be challenged or have an interviewer play the devil's advocate to see how you will respond to a different point of view.

Keep your answers short and direct. This ties into our first advice about practicing. This will help you have an idea of how lengthy and how articulate your answers are. You want to compose yourself so that your answers are short and directly relevant to the question. Refrain from rambling and avoid sidebars. You want to come across as someone thoughtful and engaged but also direct and articulate who does not have trouble conveying their thoughts. Be sure to use real-life examples and provide details to your story accurately.

Prepare some questions to ask the interviewers at the end. You want to have at least one or two questions to ask at the end of the interview so you can show that you have done your research on the school and program. Ask about how you think the campus or program differs from a nearby one or what is unique about the faculty and classroom setup. Ask about job placement and how the school works to network and place students in professional jobs after graduation. Ask about how the program has grown and developed with real-world and technological demands and what the program's biggest advantages are. Don't ask things that can easily be found out through the school's website or application page—you don't want to come off as though you haven't done your research. Ask thoughtful questions so interviewers can feel you have engaged with them and the process and are serious about considering the program for attendance.

Some Common Questions to Prepare For

Tell us a little bit about yourself.

This is an open-ended question that can lead to disorganized thoughts and rambling if you let it. Don't fall into the trap! Prepare a great, succinct two to three-minute response that focuses on your education, experiences, accomplishments, and future goals with regard to the degree you are applying for. Be articulate and structure your thoughts so you aren't bouncing all over the place. Be sure you prepare and time yourself so you have an idea of how long you have been talking.

Why do you want to earn a graduate business degree? What are your plans with it in the future?

Talk about your motivations and what you hope to accomplish with the education you will receive. Don't just focus on monetary goals but address how this degree will help you in your future plans and what doors it opens for you. Talk about your future goals and whether you are hoping to work for a firm or become an entrepreneur with the education you've gained. You want to show that you are motivated and positive about school and that you have future plans to capitalize on your education.

Why are you interested in this school/program?

Show that you've done your research on the school and program and that you really do want to be there. Talk about the rankings and accreditation of the program, the faculty, the course offerings or class sizes, the job placement record, and networking opportunities. Your conversation should reflect that you've done your homework and that this is a place that you can picture yourself belonging.

Why are you deciding to get your degree now instead of before?

This question will be common for people who have taken time off after their undergrad degree for a few gap years or to directly enter the workforce. Interviewers will be curious about why you are applying for school now and what made you take that initiative. Explain your motivations and what inspired you—whether it was a friend or family member, a supervisor at work, the economy, and demands for higher education. Share about how this will help you in your career and your goals and why you wanted to take the chance now at this particular school.

Tell us about some of your accomplishments as a leader.

Have specific examples ready that illustrate your leadership skills and how you have formed a team and taken charge to make change happen. Describe what you accomplished and what steps you took and how you made a positive impact in your school or community. The best examples would be outside of the workplace, such as a place you volunteer for community organizing. These show that you are able to take charge and lead when it comes to working with people from diverse backgrounds.

What would you describe as your strengths and what are your weaknesses?

It's very easy to talk about strengths. You can easily pick two or three that you can back up with examples from your academic or professional career. Picking a weakness can be harder because you don't want to appear weak to your interviewer or come off as too nervous or vulnerable. More than likely, the interviewer is looking to see how you handle a tough question and if you can be honest instead of arrogant. As you state a weakness, be sure to turn it into a positive as you talk about how you grew during the experience or matured from that character trait.

How will you be a positive addition to our business school campus?

Mention what you know about the campus and opportunities for clubs that appeal to you. State what you are looking forward to be involved in and how you feel you will acclimate with a diverse student body.

If you are accepted into this program, what will be your biggest challenge throughout school?

This question wants you to admit that there may be rigorous demands to the graduate program and that you are aware of what you are getting into. You don't want to come off too flippant about your responsibilities but seem like you know what a balancing act it will be to maintain a professional, personal, and academic life. Share what you are thinking about those challenges, but that you are also forming solutions on how to solve any potential problems that may occur.

What has been the most challenging experience for you that you've had to overcome?

Think about your journey, personal and professional, and about the challenges you've faced to get this far. What hurdles have you had to face to sit in this chair today? Think about those challenges that you worked through and how you made them into successful experiences. How have those phases shaped you and changed you? Use those experiences to depict an image of how you have succeeded despite obstacles and how that has shaped your motivation for further education.

What do you think about [a national or international current event]?

It's always a good idea to read up on current events before an interview so you can give a well-informed opinion about the event and its impact. Don't get too political but convey your opinion to show that you are well read and that you are aware of what's happening in the world around you. This is a great chance to share a more personal or compassionate side of yourself.

Discuss your ability to work in a team of people different from you and how you adapt to different cultures.

Talk about your diverse experiences either in the workplace, personally, or volunteering or community service. You want the interviewer to know that you value diversity and that you aren't scared of working with people who are different from you.

How would your supervisors or colleagues describe you?

Highlight positive professional and personal characteristics that are an asset to you in the workplace. Remember that your application may already contain a letter of recommendation from your supervisor, so you want to follow up on that. Don't make up an answer but elaborate on how you feel you are viewed and what traits have helped you succeed.

What do you like about your current work environment? What kind of changes would you make?

This is a great way to direct the conversation toward your work and what you are passionate about. Talk about what you love about your job and career path and what you find satisfying. Even if you are unhappy at work, you should showcase a positive attitude so the interviewer would know that you can find positivity in a negative situation. When it comes to commenting on the changes you'd make, be sure to describe how any changes would have a positive and lasting impact on the workplace. Be sure to keep your answers work-related, such as starting a group for new employees or reaching out to a new industry. This gives examples of your innovation and problem-solving skills.

What other schools are you applying to?

This can be a tricky question because you don't know how this answer will be used against you. Interviewers use this question to get a sense of your ambition and to see what other schools you are applying to. Schools want to avoid admitting candidates who seem like they have their hearts set on another school. When answering, you want to be honest and list your schools and why you chose them, such as factors including class sizes, career planning, and campus location. You should end the question with talking about why you are applying to this school and how you see it as the best fit for you. Be sure to cite specific elements of the program that appeals to you and why you are most looking forward to being admitted to this school.

Chapter 6: Strategies for Better Essay Writing

Essay writing can bring a lot of pressure, especially when it's such a heavy portion of the application process. It's a lot of stress riding on one short piece. Here we have some tips to help you become a better writer when it comes to making your application essay.

Start with an outline. Before you even start writing an essay, take some time to make a basic outline of your thoughts and how you would formulate your response. You want to be sure you are answering the question asked and you have a few examples from your life or professional career if the essay is asking for them. If you are sharing a story or an experience, be sure you are not leaving any details out. This is a great way to organize your thoughts, and then guide yourself into forming an essay.

Focus on writing an interesting essay first and then work to make it a good one. Think of your essay like a story you are sharing and work on making it an engaging one to the reader. Once you have a layout and your thoughts in place, you can edit the piece for length and structure.

Divide your essay into segments for you to focus on. Start with an introductory sentence, then a strong thesis statement, body paragraphs, and a conclusion. As you begin to divide your essay into thoughts, this can be a guide to help you have a cohesive form.

Have specific examples. If your topic is asking for examples of your leadership or team working skills, then be sure you can name specific instances. You don't want to be vague or humble because you want your strengths to shine. If you took the lead and started a program at work or you took charge where you volunteer to create a new initiative, be sure to have specific examples and talk about these instances. You want to have a clear "before and after" depiction to show how you improved things.

Have a solid understanding of basic punctuation, style, and grammar. You don't have to be an English major to write the perfect essay, but you want to be able to have the knowledge to correct your essay when necessary. Don't just leave it to your computer to point out the spelling errors for you. You should be able to make corrections where you need to. Use the active voice instead of the passive one and avoid unnecessary transition words that don't add to your structure.

Use the right vocabulary. Instead of using fancy words from the thesaurus that would require a dictionary to look them up, try and use words that are more persuasive to your cause or descriptive words if you are sharing a story. You don't want to overcompensate with big words when a simple one will do. Using larger words can sometimes just make your message harder to get across. So stay away from the thesaurus and make your first draft one that answers the essay question and shines a light on your personality.

Vary your sentence length. Even though you are writing an essay for higher education, you don't want your entire essay to be filled with heavy, overly long sentences. By switching up your sentence length, you are engaging the reader in your story and keeping them an active reader. Each sentence should contain one thought. Combining sentences together when they don't need to be, only makes it unnecessarily complex and could create confusion in the reader.

Keep your paragraphs short when you can. This is a common technique to help the reader process information easily. If you are sharing a story or telling an example of your leadership skills, then yes, a longer paragraph might be necessary. But in academic writing, you want each paragraph to contain one idea. This allows the reader to process your ideas better and see where one thought is completed and where the next begins.

Don't ramble or be redundant. Rambling can be a big problem for some writers. That's why we urge you to use our tips and outline your thoughts before beginning. You want to be sure your essay has a beginning, middle, and end, and you don't want there to be any rambling in between. Avoid repeating things you've already said before because the admission committee might have the impression that you are filling your essay with "fluff" and not having enough original material to write about. You want to be sure you have separate unique examples if asked for them so there's no overlap.

Have a strong conclusion. These are going to be the last few sentences resonating with the person reading your essay. You want the conclusion to be strong so the person ends with a great impression of you and your abilities, as well as your motivation for applying to school and how dedicated you are to your goals.

Edit, edit, and then edit again. There's no shame that your first draft isn't perfect—it's just a draft! You should edit your draft, and then edit it again. There may be things to take out, things you repeated over again, or examples you need to add to elaborate on your strengths. Have a counselor read your essay for feedback or approach family and friends to see what impression they are left with. Take a few days away from the draft and then read it again out loud to see if it successfully conveys your message without using unnecessary fluff or filler words.

Chapter 7: Know Your Audience

As you are preparing your application, agonizing over your essay, and stressing about a possible interview invite, it's important you take the time to think over who will be reviewing your application. In fact, most of the time, the person reading your MBA application might not even have an MBA. That's not to say they're not qualified, but they aren't going to be swayed by fancy technical jargon if you include it in your essay.

In fact, most admission committees might not be actual business school faculty members. They're a different group of people who work at the admission office and are trained to select the best applicants from the incoming applications. They are coached to look past any technical jargon and find the best, most authentic applicants who have a strong academic and professional background.

When you think of your top-tier business schools, you have to admit that your application is going to be just one of the thousands. Schools will often hire seasonal readers to help them wade through the pile of applications. These are people trained to find the best and unique applicants. There might be a reader looking simply at test scores to select ones who perfectly match their school. There may be a reader going over essays to find ones who have a great voice and capture a unique personality. There may be a reader simply browsing resumes to find ones who have a strong academic and professional career. There are many opportunities where you can shine, so you want to be sure all parts of your application are strong and unique to highlight your motivations and potential.

Most admission counselors are looking for sincerity and a motivation to attend their school. Yes, you are applying for a higher education graduate program, but that doesn't mean right off the bat that your essay has to be written like that. Admission officers want to see sincerity and that you have the right motivations and goals for attaining higher education. Don't "dumb yourself down" but be relatable in your essay and allow your personality and strengths to shine through.

Don't use the same resume as you would when applying for a job. Admission officers aren't necessarily looking for the jobs you've held, but they're looking at your overall skills. Communication, problem-solving, leadership, community service—these are the things that they are interested in. They will already have letters from your supervisors about your job performance. They want to know your personality beyond work. Make sure your resume is focused on explaining your skills and your strengths in the workplace and in extracurricular activities. These are the skills that admission counselors want in an incoming class so they would know if you will be a good fit for a school with a diverse student body and faculty.

Conclusion

Thank you for making it through to the end of *7 MBA Application Tips*. We hope it was informative and able to give you some tips and reduce the stress in your MBA application process. With our tips on how to select a school and a program, we hope you were able to closely look at each school on your list and see if it's right for you. Things like class size, networking opportunities, faculty interaction, and location are all important if you are going to be a full-time student at any school. By looking at a school's incoming class demographics, you can select your safety schools and target schools so you would feel comfortable with admission at any one of them. We urge you to reach for those *dream schools* because you will never know until you apply.

With our chapters on essay writing and interview preparation, we hope we were able to calm your nerves and give you tips to prepare for success. We urge you to devote some time to your essay and edit multiple drafts of it if you need to. Every draft will help you get closer to your perfect essay. You want to avoid using big words, have varying sentence lengths, and structure your essay so it includes specific examples of your success. Don't be scared to have a personal side to your essay, because it will reveal to the admission committee more about you as an individual. When it comes to an interview, we also recommend planning your thoughts concisely at home to avoid rambling in front of an interviewer. You want to dress professionally, avoid becoming too personal, and maintain a professional tone in the room. Be sure you do your research to see what interview style your school uses, whether it's a one-on-one interview or a team-based interview, this will help you feel more comfortable about the format you are going to be attending.

With our tips on standing out in a crowd of applicants, giving great impression during the interview, and making your essay the best you can, we wish you success at getting into the school of your choice!

Finally, if you found this book useful in any way, a review is always appreciated, so others can also benefit.

Garland P. Brackins

www.ingramcontent.com/pod-product-compliance
Lightning Source LLC
Chambersburg PA
CBHW030957240526
45463CB00017B/2819